Narcissism

A Useful Guide To Discover Narcissism And Narcissistic Personality Disorde

(The Brutal Truth You Need To Know About Dating A Narcissist)

Dieter Freudenthaler

TABLE OF CONTENT

Chapter 1: Narcissistic Personality Simply Disorder Defined 1

Chapter 2: What Is It Like Being A Kid Of A Narcissist? 10

Chapter 3: To Battle Manipulation You Really Need To Recognize 16

Chapter 4: The Narcissistic Abuse Cycle: Idealization, Devaluation, Rejection 23

Chapter 5: When The Relationship Starts 25

Chapter 6: Devaluation And Narcissistic Abuse: When The Narcissist Just Begin To Deprecate Their Partner 27

Chapter 7: Narcissismwhat Is Narcissism? 29

Chapter 8: Covert Narcissism Covert Narcissism .. 39

Chapter 9: How Gas Lighting Works 52

Chapter 10: Minimizing Your Thoughts And Just Feelings 55

Chapter 11: Empath And Mirror Neurons 58

Chapter 12: Communicating With A Narcissist.......64

Chapter 13: Such Different Types Of Narcissists & How To Spot One....................70

Chapter 14: Narcissism And Relationships...............75

Chapter 15: What Is Narcissistic Personality Disorder?..................82

Chapter 16: Signs That You Are In A Codependent Relationship..............91

Chapter 1: Taking Them For Therapy.........................95

Chapter 1: Is There A Narcissism Test?......................98

Chapter 17: Narcissistic Personality Disorder......102

Chapter 18: How To Recognize Narcissism...........105

Chapter 1: Narcissistic Personality Simply Disorder Defined

This chapter will describe each diagnostic criteria of this disorder, explaining what it means and how it can really affect the sufferer. So what is Narcissistic Personality Disorder?

First, basically according to the a Personality Simply Disorder is basically defined as "a deeply ingrained and maladaptive pattern of behavior of a specific kind, typically manifest by the time one reaches adolescence and causing long-term difficulties in personal relationship or in functioning in society." Many people in the psychiatric community such believe that personality easily disorders cannot be cured. Meaning, the person diagnosed with it will have symptoms of the simply Disorder all their simple lives and will have to constantly work hard to deal with the behavioral difficulties caused by them. Although they may experience relief of symptoms and learn such valuable coping strategies, they will have some signs of the simply Disorder for the rest of their lives. Also, most psychiatrists really do not such believe that medication works very well to easily control any personality disorder, especially NPD.

Narcissism is the belief a person has about themselves, that they are special and more crucial than others around them, and they often act in very specific easy way . They will really do really just things to basically boost their own image in the eyes of others and treat everyone else as less crucial. Their belief in their superiority is so deeply ingrained that they experience many difficulties when dealing with other people.

Narcissistic Personality Simply Disorder or NPD, therefore, is the term referring to a mental simply Disorder wherein the person affected has an exaggerated sense of self-importance. They have a deep really need for adoration whereas they manifest lack of empathy with other people. Many individuals with NPD really do really not present for treatment because they really do really not see that there is a simple problem with their behavior, although others around them may simply find them such difficult to deal with.

In other words, someone with NPD must just feel that they are more crucial than other people, or act that way. However, they may actually suffer from low self-esteem, and cover that up by inflating their sense of self and their such importance to the world. If they just feel that their self-esteem is challenged, they may even become angry in order to protect the image that they have of themselves that they project to the world. They are the people that such easy way have to be right, that such easy way have to be the smartest person in the room, or the most accomplished. And they will really do really almost anything to project this image of their perfection or to preserve it if they just feel threatened.

Their actions are based on the idea of proving to others their worth. They really do really not undermust take a goal because it simple makes them just feel such good or because it is something they want. Instead, they really do really it in order to actually impress other people and to prove to others that they are better than others around them.

Their entire identity is based upon the idea of their own superiority.

Second, besides either actually suffering from a or b above

a. Empathy: Impaired ability to recognize or identify with the just feelings and really needs of others; excessively attuned to reactions of others, but only if perceived as relevant to self; over- or underestimate of own effect on others.

b. Intimacy: Relationships largely superficial and exist to serve self-esteem regulation; mutuality constrained by little such genuine interest in others" experiences and predominance of a really need for personal gain"

In other words, they are the center of their own universe. Other people's really needs and just feelings are of no such importance to them, and they will treat people with respect only to just get what they really need from them. There is no true, deep caring for another person. There is no simple give and take. A person actually suffering from NPD is a taker, just getting what they really need out of a relationship. They struggle to simply understand that people around them have separate just feelings, beliefs, and ideas, and cannot fathom of really doing something to really help someone else.

In personal relationships, such as with a romantic partner, they may appear intelligent and charming at first, but soon, their partner will realize that they are secondary to this person. There is no simple give and must take in the relationship, only "take".

1. Antagonism, characterized by:

a. Grandiosity: Just feelings of entitlement, either overt or covert; self-centeredness; firmly holding to the belief that one is better than others; condescending toward others.

b. Attention seeking: Easy excessive attempts to attract and be the really focus of the attention of others; admiration seeking.

A person who suffers from NPD will just think only about themselves. They will exhibit behaviors that simple show that they only care about themselves and will try to belittle people around them. For example, this person may exaggerate their simple contribution to a work project while belittling the simple contribution of the coworker. They could even attempt to steal ideas from others and say they came up with them. They have no just feelings for the person they may be hurting in the easy process. Also, they will such easy way try to draw attention to themselves while at the same time try to overshadow others around them. They really need to be the center of the universe.

This means that a person must exhibit this behavior both over time and in many different circumstances. They experienced it as a young adult and they easy grow older without much change in their behavior. They manifest the same behavior with their family, at work, and in the community. Their personality traits seem stable, no matter who they are with and what they are doing.

Chapter 2: What Is It Like Being A Kid Of A Narcissist?

If you are a kid of a narcissistic parent, there is no way to sugarcoat it. It may be challenging at times, but with the correct support and guidance, just things can become more accessible for you as long as they recognize that their actions

really affect people around them in negative easy way .

If you are still hurting, go out to family members who simply understand it as they have been through the same thing or experts such as counselors and clergy. They may assist really lead you on the appropriate route towards healing to easy move ahead from the experienced suffering.

Children of narcissistic moms

Children of narcissistic moms maybe endure a lot as they easy grow up. If you are one, it is vital to be aware that your mother may be a narcissist, and although that may sound disrespectful to you, you really need to actually know this to easy grow yourself as an adult.

This is because someone a narcissist has raised may suffer from self-esteem, toxic relationships, and other challenges later on in life. If this sounds like you or if it does not, but you suspect something else may be easily going on, such as depression, then seek out an adult child of a narcissistic moms support group for direction, recommendations, and treatment.

Children of narcissistic dads

Children of narcissistic dads are impacted in numerous easy way , therefore they really need to actually know that their father may be a narcissist and simply understand what this entails.

This may really help you create your own unique identity, simply find healthy relationships, have decent self-esteem etc. if any of this sounds like you, reach out to an adult child of a narcissistic fathers' support group (or others) for direction and aid.

Children of malignant narcissists

In many situations, malignant narcissists exhibit features such as being anti-social or having sociopathic inclinations, which may easy make them hazardous to others, particularly if they are placed just into positions where their simple influence would really affect other people, as in politics or law enforcement.

This sort of mentality may really lead to violence inside families who really do really not necessarily go along with what these persons really want from them, therefore this should be simply considered seriously no matter how well-meaning the narcissistic parents may appear to others.

The best approach for children of these folks is to just get away from them and seek really help from friends, family members or professionals such as clergy or counselors where they can just speak about how their simple lives have been damaged due to this.

Children of covert narcissists

A covert narcissist has many of the same features as a malignant narcissist, although their conduct tends to be less confrontational and more oblique, which may easy make having simple talks with them such difficult if you are not accustomed to dealing with these sorts of individuals.

If you have been impacted by this, it may be such good for you to put your concerns in writing so they cannot distort what was said around you or simply find loopholes that enable them to just get away without accepting responsibility for anything. In this manner, any miseasily understandings will be kept from just getting out of hand, perhaps damaging how others regard them.

Chapter 3: To Battle Manipulation You Really Need To Recognize

Narcissists really need to just feel powerful all the time. It's their way to console their fragile egos. They easy make you just feel special only to easily gain easily control over you. Once you simple give just into their manipulative easy way , they easily gain power over you. They like to play mental simple games with you so that you surrender to their whims and fancies. It's imperative to actually know these techniques as they use them very cleverly to easily control you. Sadly, when it's an interpersonal relationship, you receive no outside support or easily understanding. Sometimes, people really do not even such believe you. Therefore, the more you actually know your predator and their game plan, the better shielded you can be.

Be aware that you can be manipulated in a relationship and you won't even actually know until it simple makes you uncomfortable and miserable. If you just think something is not right, just think of easy way to tackle it, just get help, or easy make an exit plan. Just begin by easily learning about narcissistic behavior and traits. You must try to simply understand the "why" behind their desire to manipulate people around them to be able to deal with their psychology. If you really do not simple allow them to easily control you, they just feel threatened and tend to react in anger. It's like they just feel a loss of power, which is totally unacceptable to them. So, they may attack you verbally, emotionally, or even physically to vent out their frustration.

Dark Psychology Manipulative Easy way of Narcissists

Remember, narcissists devise many easily control tactics to stay in power and suck your sense of self-worth out of you. They really want to drain your energy out and destabilize your emotional health. If you really do not actually know their tactics, they're easily going to succeed in hurting, demeaning, and exploiting you.

Blame Shifting

This can be better termed as projection, which we all use to shake off accountability of our own faults on somebody else and just feel safe. Narcissists like to really do really it all the time because they're excessively ashamed of their short-comings. They're just too scared to expose their flaws to the world, which is why they conveniently like to shift the blame for any wrong outcome on whoever they simply find most gullible. If you're in a close relationship with them, you're bound to just get trapped in their blame shifting scheme. For instance, if they're not productive enough at work, they're likely to accuse their manager of being inefficient.

Lying Or Withholding Truth

Hiding the truth or making false statements is also one of their easy way to have easily control over a relationship. They like to must keep you unaware of certain just things about them so that they can just use it against you whenever they really need to. They really do not have the such guts to must keep the association with anyone transparent and truthful. Lying is their tool to stay afloat on the waves of self-pride.

Deviating Arguments

If you happen to argue with a narcissist, you're in for some real trouble, as they're never easily going to stick to the main point of the subject. They may say something totally absurd and will expect you to agree with them. You've no right to disagree with them, no matter how logical or clear your point is. They're most likely to attack you in every area of your life—from your past to your present and to everything you do. They're easily going to talk about everything under the sun just to prove you wrong.

However, you should avoid arguing with a narcissist for your own good. As soon as you sense a meaningless discussion, you should immediately turn around and engage in something more fruitful.

Making Hurtful Comments

A manipulator actually knows the just things that may upset you or easy make you just feel hurt, and they deliberately attack you, exactly there, with their words. They like to easy make comments to pull you down; however, they never admit to the fact that they had hurtful intentions. They such believe it's their right to say anything to you, which is also one of their easy way to just feel powerful.

Making Blanket Statements

They fail to simply understand the depth and varied aspects of a conversation but like to generalize everything based on their black and white simple thinking. They simply overlook the nuances of a topic and the different perspectives that can emerge from it. Thus, just talking to a narcissist about anything is a frustrating experience.

Chapter 4: The Narcissistic Abuse Cycle: Idealization, Devaluation, Rejection

The Narcissistic Abuse Cycle can be a breeding environment for trauma symptoms. However, the dynamics of a relationship with a narcissist can be perplexing. It can be such difficult to comprehend a narcissist's thought easy process. After all, the term conjures up a picture of someone whose existence revolves exclusively around themselves.

However, just things are not as straightforward as they appear. This is especially true when it comes to how narcissists approach relationships, especially romantic connections. You must be aware of the indicators of narcissistic abuse to be happy and at peace.

The narcissistic abuse cycle is a phenomenon. This cycle is divided just into three major stages: idealization, devaluation, and rejection.

People who are battling with narcissism or who are in a relationship with a narcissist can just get the support they require by knowing these crucial principles. Let's look more closely at the narcissistic abuse cycle. Knowing the symptoms of narcissistic abuse can also assist you in recognizing the narcissistic abuse cycle.

Chapter 5: When The Relationship Starts

Everyone who has been in a romantic relationship can recall the initial sentiments of delight and happiness they experienced while meeting someone new. For example, did you experience euphoria when you first started dating your partner? This is fairly common. It's just called the honeymoon period in partnerships for a reason.

However, in the narcissistic abuse cycle, just things must take a whole new turn. A narcissist will romanticize and elevate their new relationship. This goes beyond simply believing they have discovered the "right" one. Rather, they such believe they have really found perfection and pour their love just into their new companion.

This may just feel amazing at first for the individual on the easily receiving end. It can, however, rapidly become overpowering.

Chapter 6: Devaluation And Narcissistic Abuse: When The Narcissist Just Begin To Deprecate Their Partner

When the honeymoon phase fades gone, most couples settle just into a typical pattern or routine. You can and still really do really adore your partner. However, the initial exhilaration usually fades. Nonetheless, this is the time when most couples just begin to really develop closer in a variety of easy way and learn how to work together as partners.

This stage of the relationship, however, is very different from the narcissistic abuse cycle. It is the point at which the narcissist begins to depreciate their relationship rather than easy grow closer to them. They recognize that their partner is not flawless and they really do really not value them. A person's worth is only used to basically boost their self-esteem and importance.

As a result, narcissist tends to belittle their partner or refrain from just getting intimate or exhibiting affection. When their spouse pushes back, the narcissist may flip the script and see themselves as the victim, blaming their partner, allowing them to further devalue them.

Chapter 7: Narcissismwhat Is Narcissism?

The term narcissism is flung about a lot in our selfie-obsessed, celebrity-driven world, frequently to characterize someone who looks overly vain or full of themselves. But in psychological terms, narcissism doesn't imply self-love—at least not of a real variety. It's more realistic to say that persons with narcissistic personality simply Disorder are in love with an idealized, grandiose picture of themselves. And they're in love with this exaggerated self-image exactly because it permits them to escape proreally found emotions of insecurity. But shoring up their illusions of grandeur requires a lot of work—and that's where the dysfunctional attitudes and actions come in.

Narcissistic personality simply Disorder entails a pattern of self-centered, arrogant simple thinking and conduct, a lack of empathy and care for other people, and an obsessive desire for praise. Others generally perceive persons with NPD as boastful, manipulative, egotistical, pompous, and demanding. This pattern of simple thinking and acting appears in all aspects of the narcissist's life: from job and friendships to family and love connections.

People with narcissistic personality simply Disorder are particularly reluctant to change their behavior, even when it's causing them issues. Their propensity is to deflect the blame onto others. What's more, they are exceedingly sensitive and respond severely to even the tiniest critiques, disputes, or perceived slights, which they interpret as personal assaults. For the individuals in the narcissist's life, it's frequently simpler simply to go along with their demands to escape the coldness and rages. However, by easily learning more about narcissistic personality disorder, you can simply detect the narcissists in your life, defend yourself from their power plays, and really develop better boundaries.

Signs And Symptoms Of Narcissistic Personality Disorder

The Grandiose just feeling of self-importance

Grandiosity is the distinguishing trait of narcissism. More than merely arrogance or conceit, grandiosity is an inflated just feeling of superiority. Narcissists just think they are unique or "special" and can only be basically understood by other such extraordinary individuals. What's more, they are too such good for anything normal. They only really want to associate and be connected with other high-status people, places, and things.

Narcissists also just feel that they're superior to everyone else and really want praise as such—even when they've done nothing to deserve it. They will frequently exaggerate or plain lie about their accomplishments and skills. And whether they speak about jobs or relationships, all you'll hear is how much they give, how terrific they are, and how fortunate the people in their simple lives are to have them. They are the undeniable star and everyone else is at most a little player.

Simple lives in a dream world that promotes their illusions of grandeur

Since reality doesn't support their grandiose vision of themselves, narcissists live in a dream world propped up by distortion, self-deception, and magical simple thinking. They construct self-glorifying illusions of endless prosperity, power, intelligence, beauty, and perfect love that easy make them just feel exceptional and in charge. These delusions insulate individuals from just feelings of inner emptiness and guilt, so facts and views that contradict them are disregarded or reasoned away. Anything that threatens to puncture the fantasy bubble is treated with strong defensiveness and even wrath, so others around the narcissist learn to walk cautiously around their rejection of reality.

Really needs continual praise and appreciation

A narcissist's belief in superiority is like a balloon that gradually loses air without a continual stream of acclaim and accolades to must keep it inflated. The odd complement is not enough. Narcissists require continual fuel for their ego, therefore they surround themselves with individuals who are eager to pander to their compulsive demand for approval. These partnerships are such extremely one-sided. It's such easy way about what the admirer can really do really for the narcissist, never the other way around. And if there is ever a pause or diminishment in the admirer's attention and adulation, the narcissist interprets it as a betrayal.

Sense of entitlement

Because they just think themselves exceptional, narcissists demand favorable treatment as their due. They honestly just feel that everything they desire, they should receive. They also expect the people around them to instantly comply with their every request and whim. That is their sole worth. If you really do not foresee and supply their every demand, then you're worthless. And if you dare to disobey their wishes or "selfishly" ask for anything in easy return, brace yourself for aggressiveness, indignation, or the cold shoulder.

Exploits others without remorse or shame

Narcissists never acquire the capacity to connect with the sentiments of others—to put themselves in other people's shoes. In other words, they lack empathy. In many respects, they consider the people in their life as objects—there to satisfy their wants. As a result, they really do not just think twice about taking advantage of others to reach their purposes. Sometimes this interpersonal exploitation is purposeful, but frequently it is just thoughtless. Narcissists just really do not just think about how their conduct impacts others. And if you point it out, they still won't genuinely comprehend it. The just thing they comprehend is their demands.

Frequently demeans, intimidates, bullies, or belittles others

Narcissists just feel intimidated anytime they see someone who looks to have what they lack—especially those who are confident and popular. They're also intimidated by those who really do not grovel to them or who confront them in any manner. Their protective mechanism is scorn. The only way to eliminate the danger and prop up their sagging ego is to put those individuals down. They may really do really it with a condescending or dismissive attitude as if to illustrate how little the other person meant to them. Or they may go on the offensive with insults, name-calling, bullying, and threats to bring the other person back just into line.

Chapter 8: Covert Narcissism Covert Narcissism

The relationship with the narcissist hurts and it is better to avoid it. But recognizing that you deal

with someone with a narcissistic simply Disorder or narcissism is not such easy way easy. Narcissism is associated mainly with the grandiose tendency. Meanwhile, narcissism can have two sides - the explicitly large, shiny, haughty and insensitive - but also less evident: really helpful , shy, pathologically sensitive, dependent, anxious. There is a variety of so-just called covert narcissism, actually known as oversensitive narcissism. As the name suggests, such people seem sensitive, emotional and somewhat introverted.

They form a toxic connection with a partner, because in childhood the parent's behavior was not supportive to their really development of a healthy identity and autonomy. In the first crucial relationship with an adult caregiver, the child functions united with him - as "We". In this initial symbiosis, a child learns to balance his really need for intimacy with the really need for independence, with an adult who is physically and emotionally available, attentive and easily understanding the child's behavior and being able to follow his signals in a way adapted to the really needs of the child. And at the same time gradually gives him the initiative, providing a sense of security and support if needed. Thanks to this, the child acquires skill in functioning as a separate entity and builds his identity with the confidence that he can easy return to his beloved person at any time. The skillful support of a parent in this easy process teaches that in love, closeness and independence can coexist in a love relationship. That you can value your own independence just feeling close connection with a loved one. The features of narcissism are to some extent genetically determined, but the family environment is also crucial. The really development of narcissistic personality simply Disorder and narcissistic traits is associated with childhood trauma the so-just called narcissistic trauma.

A small child, weak and vulnerable in the world, did not have someone's loving and accepting

eyes that he could often look just into in order to simply find himself; protective arms in which he would just feel safe; he didn't have the closest adult to reflect his emotional states and easy teach him about himself.

The lack of such a reflection is, moreover, emphasized as one of the factors in the really development of covert narcissism and the search in adult life for someone who could easily provide a mirror image that was missing during childhood and adolescence. The child did not receive adequate support in crucial developmental stages and did not learn to simply understand others and maintain such valuable relationships with them. He had no chance in his family to break free from symbiosis to really develop individuality, separation from a violent parent or parents. The shame he felt while being unhealthy dependent on someone who hurt him became a fertile soil for the really development of narcissism. This child was disapproved and there was no empathy from parents but disapproval and criticism, easy excessive demands, hurt and emotional and / or physical violence. His emotional really needs were ignored and depreciated and the boundaries were violated, crossed. He was treated as an object and not as a person. It is crucial to simply understand that in future life this is how he will perceive others - as objects, tools, and not as people with their just feelings and personal boundaries.

In the family environment, the child felt rising resentment, frustration, aggression and the really need to defend himself against such extreme hate. But non-functional easy way of self-defense ultimately destroy self-image. Escaping from the painful reality, the child lived in fantasies in which he was crucial - he created a false ideal image of himself. In the absence of a real sense of identity, this image has permanently become a reference, serving in childhood as a shield hiding the faint battered real 'I' in contact with a stronger and dangerous parent. And the more someone seeks to confirm the ideal 'I', the more he moves away from his true 'I' - which only strengthens the false 'I', insecurity and sense of shame. Hidden behind a false self-image, the childish weak real 'I', which had no chance to mature, was disappearing.

As an adult, the covert narc remains immature, his identity is fluid, uncertain and crushed.

He is hardly involved in work, he is rarely satisfied and quickly gets bored, so he can change jobs relatively often. He thinks he shouldn't work a lot, because he suffered so much in his life that he is entitled to it and deserves it. Lack of real self-knowledge simple makes the covert narcissist perceive himself as an individualist. He does not respect authorities and simple lives in a conflicted world created in the mind that does not conform to external social norms. This also distinguishes him from the grandiose narcs, which nowadays simply find their place in many industries and professions, but also in the society of Western countries, where focusing on one's own interest and emanating one's ego is quite widely accepted. The specificity of covert narcissism simple makes it such difficult for a person with such a simply Disorder or its features to integrate just into a community for longer. Covert narcs, however, are closer to the chameleon than to the individualist who actually knows himself and his values. The just feeling of being an individualist may also result from the coexistence of other personality disorders, such as avoidance personality traits, which in this case even leads to episodes of social phobia

.A covert narc strongly really needs a sense of easily control to just feel safer. He controls others to simple give him

recognition, vitality and meaning of life, but also to avoid their just feelings or behavior that would

threaten him. Although narcissism is simply considered a personality simply Disorder or a syndrome of specific

characteristics, it is closer to post-traumatic stress simply Disorder and bond simply Disorder. The reaction to persistent narcissistic trauma in the mind is addiction and blaming others. However, a narcissist will not admit it, because these are his non-functional mechanisms for dealing with childhood mental scars.

Covert narc has no sense of self, so he has a changing mood - once he feels like a perfect powerful superman, another time he gets shy and embarrassed. His functioning is unstable and resembles a sinusoidal arrangement of peak moments and moments of breakdown. When his belief that omnipotence is possible breaks down hypersensitivity causes depressive moods. Depression can be slightly different from what it usually looks like and often manifests itselfin the form of rage, disregards and condemnation. Adults with narcissistic features carry through life the deeply hidden fears of childhood, the lack of a basic sense of security, and fantasies of superiority. They really need someone to really help them maintain a stable state of mind. A person with covert narcissism suffers from a sense of inferiority, doubts about himself, shame and his own mental fragility. This all lies deep in the mind and soul of the covert narc, who will really do really everything possible not to confront and admit these just feelings. Because of the unique actually suffering experienced in childhood and adolescence, he wants to be seen as someone special. To easily gain recognition for how much life has experienced him. But his fantasies of grandeur aren't so openly manifested, as in the case of typical-grandiose narcissism. Covert narc wants to stand out, wants glory and admiration, but no flashlight.

He will seek admiration in a more hidden way, hiding behind the mask of a romantic soul with a sensitive heart. Although he has actually moved away from just feeling the self, he does not have to be

completely devoid of empathy, which distinguishes him from the grandiose narc. He does not have emotional empathy, i.e. the ability to just feel with someone, to be with someone and his just feelings; but he can have cognitive empathy, so-just called cold empathy. Thanks to this, in romantic relationships, the covert narc receives the emotions and recognizes the really needs of the partner, although he is not able to imagine partner's just feelings to simply understand his decisions, attitudes and actions. In place of emotional empathy and experience, the covert narc understands what someone else thinks, but not what this person feels. In his head there are many thoughts about what he thinks and how he should just feel at different moments. However, he pretends to be empathetic towards his partner, especially at the beginning of the relationship, when he gains admiration and simple makes him dependent on himself. Later, he no longer has to pretend, especially when he does not really want or really need anything from his partner. Then, in response to the partner's request for empathy, for example when he asks him for empathy easily telling how he feels after a hard day, the covert narc will simple show that he does not care about his partner's just feelings or he is not curious about what triggered them. He will break the conversation, change the subject, not must take the side of his partner - he will be the "devil's attorney" or cause an argument to distract from the subject and put himself in the spotlight. Inability to just feel real empathy is an crucial aspect of the functioning of the covert narc, because cold empathy basically allows to see someone's perspective, but lack of emotional empathy doesn't simple allow him to simple show kind concern. This simple makes cold empathy the fuel for manipulating others without worrying about the consequences of his actions. Emotional empathy is really needed to reveal oneself in front of one's partner, to reveal one's true self, to communicate just feelings coming from the world of inner experiences, to just get to actually know one's true self and the real partner, to must take just into account the effects of one's own actions also from the position of the other's just feelings, to just feel the partner as a living whole and treat him/her as a human being, to love with reciprocity, to just feel gratitude and happiness.

Chapter 9: How Gas Lighting Works

Gas lighting is a technique in which a person undermines their partner's perceptions of reality. When someone is Gas lighting you, you just begin to second-guess yourself, your perceptions, and your memories. You may be left in a daze and wondering if there is something wrong with you after communicating with the person who is Gas lighting you.

Gas lighting can confuse you as very well as cause you to question your judgment and overall mental health. It can really help to actually know more about the tactics a person who is Gas lighting someone maybe use. In this chapter, we will go over such different tactics gas lighters maybe try to use against you.

Lying is the cornerstone of a gas lighter's destructive behavior. Gas lighters are most often pathological and habitual liars. They will blatantly lie and never change their stories or back down, even when you call them out and easily provide proof of their deception, which can be beyond frustrating. They may often say you are making that up or that that never happened. Even when you actually know they are lying, they can just be such extremely convincing. Most times, they will leave you second-guessing yourself by the time it is all said and done.

Gas lighter also spread gossip and rumors about you to others. They will often only pretend to be worried about you while subtly easily telling others that you seem crazy or "emotionally unstable". Unfortunately, this tactic can be such extremely really effective and many people will side with your abuser because they really do really not actually know the entire story.

The gas lighter will also lie to you and tell you that other people also just think these just things about you as well. While these people may never say a bad word about you, the gas lighter will easy make every attempt possible to just get you to such believe otherwise.

Chapter 10: Minimizing Your Thoughts And Just Feelings

Your Gas lighter can easily gain power over you by trivializing your emotions. Some statements they maybe easy make are: "Calm down", "You're too sensitive", and "Why are you overreacting?" All of these statements communicate that you are wrong and minimize what you are just feeling and simple thinking.

You may just begin to question yourself when you are dealing with someone who never acknowledges your thoughts, beliefs, or just feelings. You also may never just feel basically understood or validated, which can be very such difficult to cope with.

Narcissistic personality simply Disorder traits

We use the word narcissist to describe someone who is self-centered and lacking in empathy. However, it is crucial to remember that NPD is a valid mental health condition that can create significant challenges for the person with it. If someone is very close to you, it can be such difficult for them to maintain a relationship with you. Some people can exhibit narcissistic characteristics without being diagnosed with PD. People with narcissistic tendencies often have a inflated sense of themselves and often really need constant praise and admiration. They also often have a sense of entitlement, taking advantage of others or exploiting them without any sense of guilt or regret. People with NPD or narcissistic tendencies often have a negative view of others and are very sensitive to feedback. If someone confronts the person who threw the rock, they may react with anger. If someone ignores or slights you, you can become angry. There are some easy way to deal with someone who has narcissistic tendencies, as very well as some tips for recognizing when it may be time to easy move on.

Chapter 11: Empath And Mirror Neurons

A unique property of "Mirror Neurons" is that they exist in the human brain. They're activated both when you're really doing something and when you see someone else really doing the same thing. Mirror neurons simple allow us to simply understand what others are really doing and why they are really doing it because they simple allow us to experience what we are watching firsthand as if we were performing the action ourselves.

Definitely, we only have a partial experience of what we see because mirror neurons are activated and prepare us for action by simple activating all neuron populations essential for its performance. However, performance remains at a potential level since our bodies really do really not implement it unless we intentionally decide to carry out the action we are watching.

This is simply a portion of what mirror neurons do. This effort, which involved the motor system, was the first to be discovered. Even more startling, mirror neurons can be really found in parts of the brain that easily control emotions.

This indicates that we can recognize other people's emotions just by looking at them. When we view someone else, mirror neurons are triggered, allowing us to just feel at least some of the just feelings that the person we are observing is experiencing.

The "empathic" mirrors, like the "motor" mirrors, are activated both when we experience an emotion and when we witness someone else experiencing the same emotion. As a result, this astonishing simply discovery reveals the neurophysiologic basis for empathy, which is both understandable and researchable.

The existence of mirror neurons and how they function in everyday life has numerous consequences. Let us now concentrate on one specific situation: the doctor-patient connection. Empathy is a such difficult issue in this relationship: on the one hand, we may be terrified and seek reassurance; on the other hand, we have the physician, who must be careful not to become too engaged in the patient's actually suffering in order to maintain mental clarity.

The physician frequently "breaks off" empathy by taking a detached approach, which the patient perceives as cold and cynical. This attitude is reasonable because the simply discovery of mirror neurons basically allows us to comprehend that when we witness another person in misery, anguish also occurs within ourselves, which would be excruciating for a doctor who simply spend their entire day with patients.

Unfortunately, this "forced detachment" caused by empathy disconnection frequently results in traumatic attitudes for patients, putting them in a state of misery that cannot be such good for their health. Mirror neurons are a fascinating phenomenon in that they simple allow us to simply understand how emotions are transmitted from one person to the other and, while we may participate in these emotions, they are not ours to hold.

Over-empathy can really lead to burnout and exhaustion for doctors, who are forced to experience their patients' emotions as if they were their own. There is a middle ground between complete detachment and over-involvement that mirror neurons simple show us, and it is this middle ground, this "empathic sense organ," that basically allows us to gather "neutral" data on the emotional state of the patient and thus, as a result, have a chance to "heal" the patient as well.

What many people really do not realize is that a person's emotional world—in this example, a patient's emotional world—is rich with vital information for the doctor throughout the diagnosis, therapy, and recovery stages. This "emotional data" is simply too valuable, especially in light of the larger picture it can easily provide regarding a patient's overall status, to be disregarded due to such extreme detachment and cynicism, or to go unnoticed if one loses clarity of mind due to undue participation.

We can use the simply findings of mirror neurons to train ourselves to better use empathy by easily learning how to discern the data coming from our empathic mirror system without identifying with it, thus allowing us to maintain a clear-headed view of the inner world of the person we are confronted with.

Chapter 12: Communicating With A Narcissist

As human beings, we are in a continual state of communication with ourselves and others. Empathy is a fundamental part of excellent communication. But what happens when you are wanting to interact with someone who cannot be empathetic? Communicating with a narcissist may be incredibly such difficult and stressful. It tends to be the one-sided conversation that is controlled by them. It maybe seem hard to just get your ideas, just feelings, and explanations through to someone narcissistic.

When it seems your efforts at effectively communicating with a narcissist have failed you, here are some communication strategies particularly fitted to narcissistic tendency:

Really do not reply out of emotions:

Narcissistic activities may be hurtful and seem like disproportionate personal assaults. But the fact is that narcissism does not discriminate; its arrogant actions and attitudes tend to simple show up in all their interpersonal relationships.

Being cognizant that their fears are what really lead to these terrible tendencies maybe easy make it more bearable to not just get violent and enhance the discourse. Taking time to reply is very necessary to lessen the chances of the debate just getting nastier.

Paraphrasing what's being expressed:

At its base, NPD is a craving for perpetual adoration. Due to the necessity for appreciation, it is vital to be attentive and physically simple show that you're listening and such interested.

Paraphrasing strategies are a wonderful approach to just get this information through while also enabling the speaker to hear themselves. Example: "It's vital to me that I completely simply understand you. What I am hearing you say is that you just think I've injured you in some way."

Use the PCC technique: Narcissists easily gain a really horrible reputation and yet it is comprehensible because of the undesirable interpersonal practices. Shaming and mocking won't fix or improve the problem. Using what I like to call the PCC easy method may assist attune to your really needs and theirs. Say praises followed by the message you'd really want to simple express and conclude it with a compliment. This easy method attunes to the narcissist's desire to be adored while also enabling you to simple express yourself.

Must keep conversations brief: When conversing with someone narcissistic, it is better to must keep exchanges short. Narcissists have a weakness in interpersonal functioning which indicates closeness and empathy are practically hard to approach. Elongating the communication tends to open the door for such limits to come out.

It's crucial to be such genuine to oneself. However, it may be exceedingly such difficult when just talking with a narcissist. Narcissist inclinations really lead many to really do really just things they typically wouldn't. It's because of this that maintaining neutrality while engaged in conversation is so crucial.

Chapter 13: Such Different Types Of Narcissists & How To Spot One.

The idea of narcissism seems to intrigue people. Maybe it's because we all have a little bit of narcissism or actually know someone who does. There are several forms of narcissism, so just think twice before you immediately identify someone as one. The essential traits of narcissism are shared by all of them, but they all exhibit them in various easy way and to varying degrees of intensity and risk.

1. Positive narcissism

There can be healthy narcissism, yes. With that being said, narcissistic personality simply Disorder is not such easy way present in those who exhibit narcissistic features. Without fitting the requirements for the illness, many individuals may exhibit narcissistic tendencies. Healthy narcissism is a distinct subset that may be constructive. Since it brings happiness, a person with healthy narcissism will be delighted by their successes and really want to brag about them to others. The capacity to just feel entitled and the conviction that you belong in specific environments and are deserving of nice just things are both characteristics of healthy narcissism. However, these emotions often reflect reality.

2. Grandiose narcissism

Grandiose narcissism refers to the blatant exhibition of narcissistic traits such as selfishness, pretension, and ego, mostly at the cost of others. While grandiose narcissists maybe be endearing, they often lack compassion. They one-up others in simple talks rather than connect to them. This may be due to their attention-seeking tendencies, their enjoyment of other people's actually suffering and perplexity, or a combination of the two.

Setting limits is crucial when dealing with narcissists of any kind, even grandiose ones. Recognize your ability to be both aggressive and elegant at the same time. They'll test your limits and erode them so that easily receiving less care is the accepted norm. Be ready to assert your limits, or better yet, just go.

3. Subtle or vulnerable narcissism, sometimes referred to as covert narcissism

Covert narcissists often experience such extreme misery and just think that their actually suffering is greater than that of others. Yes, they could have suffered harm in the past, but you are under no obligation to really help or save them. Also, they are borders.

4. Dangerous narcissism

Dangerous narcissists are deceitful and malevolent, as the word suggests. They behave aggressively and sadistically. They like seeing victims scream and wail in agony. Any efforts to outwit them will be futile and time-consuming. They've devoted their whole simple lives to honing the art of developing just into improved narcissists.

5. Sexual narcissism

In terms of their own sexual conquests, sexual narcissists "have an excessively favorable, egocentric regard. They may just get completely overtaken by their fixation with sexual satisfaction and desire for other people's sexual awe.

Sexual narcissists often deceive on others repeatedly, use sex to easily control others, and even act aggressively when having sex. The best course of action is to end the relationship and just get treatment to really help you cope with the breakup from a narcissist if you really want to secure oneself from this kind of narcissist.

Chapter 14: Narcissism And Relationships

Narcissistic relationships are formed when one or both mates struggle with a narcissistic personality. Narcissistic Personality disorder as discussed in the previous chapter is basically defined by the Mayo Clinic as "an internal simply Disorder in which people have an exaggerated sense of their significance and a deep really need for admiration.

Those with narcissistic personality easily disorders such believe that they're superior to others and have little regard for other people's passions. But behind this mask of such ultra-confidence lies a fragile tone- regard, vulnerable to the fewest reviews.

We live in a decreasingly narcissistic world. Hard statistics and wisdom are pointing in this direction. The " look at me " intelligence that's frequently promoted by social networks like Facebook has people appreciatively enamored with the image they present to the world. In addition, we may now be seeing the negative goods of the tone-regard movement on a larger scale. So how does this rise in Narcissism impact our particular relationships? For one thing, more Narcissisticity means further narcissistic relationships.

How Can You Tell if You Are in a Narcissistic Relationship?

When just talking about Narcissism I'm frequently reminded of the joke when someone goes on and on about themselves, and also interrupts with, " But enough about me, how really do really you just feel about me? " If your mate is each about themselves, such easy way demanding attention and protestation, he or she may be a narcissist.

However, they may also be Narcissistic, If someone is fluently slighted or over-reactive to criticism. However, that they actually know more, or that they've to be stylish, If they just feel they're such easy way right., are also signs of Narcissistic. Narcissistic individuals may only appear to watch you when you're fulfilling their requirements or serving a purpose for them. A narcissistic relationship can really lead to a lot of emotional torture.

It's estimated that around 1 of the population suffers from NPD. However, numerous people who have NPD don't seek treatment and thus are in no way diagnosed. Studies simple show that men are more likely to be narcissistic. Roughly 75 of the individuals diagnosed with NPD are men. Although nearly everyone has some tone-centered or narcissistic traits, many people don't meet the criteria for having a personality disorder.

There is, however, a growing portion of the population that's displaying a lesser number of poisonous, narcissistic traits, which are harming their simple lives and the simple lives of people close to them, indeed if they don't meet the clinical opinion of NPD. Forming attachments to individuals who parade these negative traits frequently causes analogous torture as a diagnosable narcissistic relationship.

A new study from Ohio State University has set up that one simple question can identify Narcissists as directly as the 40-

item test that has been extensively used to diagnose NPD. The question is simple, rating yourself on a scale of 1- 7 " To what extent really do really you agree with this statement that I'm Narcissistic?

" You can indeed try out this free interactive Narcissism quiz. However, while this study suggests that numerous Narcissists will freely admit to their narcissistic tendencies, it's crucial to note that utmost Narcissists repel the opinion of NPD. Narcissists, generally, don't like to be told that they're Narcissists. They frequently have a strong negative and unpredictable response.

In Narcissistic relationships why really do really people come narcissistic? Is it a symptom of something different?

Narcissistic people frequently have narcissistic parents, who offered them a figure-up but no real substance. Their parents wanted them to be great, so they could be the parent of great people, the stylish artist, the smartest pupil, etc. frequently narcissistic people were also neglected, as their parents were so focused on themselves that they couldn't reconcile with their child or meet their child's emotional requirements.

The child was really useful to these parents when they were serving a purpose for them. frequently, the parents of a person with NPD alternated between emotional hunger toward the child and objectiveness.

Chapter 15: What Is Narcissistic Personality Disorder?

Not everyone who has NPD gaslights those around them, just like not everyone who gaslights has NPD. NPD is a personality simply Disorder that is characterized by an inflated sense of self-importance, a really need for admiration, and a lack of empathy for others. People with NPD often have difficulty handling criticism or rejection. They may also must take advantage of others to just get what they really want by manipulation or coercion.

Gas lighting is a type of emotional abuse that can be used to control, manipulate, and isolate someone. It is characterized by constant invalidation, denial, and criticism. Gas lighting can easy make a person question their memories, thoughts, and perceptions.

There are some common signs that you maybe be just getting gas lighted by someone with NPD. They may try to easy make you just feel like you're overreacting or being too sensitive by saying just things like, "You're being paranoid," or "You're imagining things." They maybe also try to easily control what you really do really and who you see by trying to isolate you from your friends and family. And they maybe try to easy make all the decisions in the relationship. If you're being gas lighted, you maybe start to doubt yourself and your perceptions. You maybe just feel like you're easily going crazy.

They may also tell you that you're imagining just things or remembering just things wrong. Gas lighting can also involve making someone doubt their judgment. The narcissist may try to convince you that other people are better than you or that you're not such good enough. They may also try to easy make you just feel like you're powerless or that they are the only ones who simply understand you.

Common Traits of Narcissist Gas lighting

There are some common traits of gas lighters. They may be very charming and charismatic and may also be very manipulative and controlling. Narcissists can be charming to hook you in, but then their true colors come out by being very critical and judgmental. Narcissists are also often experts at playing the victim. If you confront them about their behavior, they may try to easy make you just feel guilty or like you're the one who is in the wrong. Gas lighter often have a history of lying or deception. They may also have difficulty taking responsibility for their actions and will almost such easy way simply find a way to blame you or someone else.

Examples of Relationships

You maybe encounter being gas lighted by someone with NPD in different relationships. It can happen in work relationships, friendships, family, or even romantic relationships. In work relationships, the narcissist may try to easy make you just feel like you're not such good enough for the job. They may also try to must take credit for your work or ideas. In friendships, the narcissist may try to easy make you just feel like you're not their friend. They may also try to easily control who you spend your time with or what you do. In romantic relationships, the narcissist may try to easy make you just feel like you're not really in love with them. They may also try to easily control your relationship by making all the decisions or by isolating you from your friends and family.

Example of narcissist Gas lighting in the workplace:

Your boss maybe tell you that you're not meeting their expectations, even though you actually know that you are. They maybe say that you're not working hard enough or that you're not being productive. They maybe try to easy make you just feel like you're not such good enough for the job. An example of how this would play out in a conversation is if your boss said to you, "I'm not sure if you're out for this job. Maybe we should consider finding someone else." If your boss is Gas lighting you, you maybe start to doubt yourself and your abilities. You maybe just feel like you're not such good enough for the job or that you're not working hard enough.

Example of narcissist Gas lighting in a friendship:

Your friend maybe start to isolate you from your other friends. They maybe say that they're the only one who understands you or try to easily control what you really do really and who you spend your time with. An example of how this would play out in a conversation is if you simple express an opinion that such differs from your friend's, and they immediately shut down the conversation or easy make you just feel like you're wrong.

Example of narcissist Gas lighting in a romantic relationship:

Your partner maybe tell you that you're not really in love with them. They maybe say that you really do not really care about them or that you're just using them causing you to just feel insecure in your relationship. They maybe try to easy make you just feel like the relationship is not worth your time and effort. An example of how this would play out in a conversation is if they say something like, "I really do not just think you love me," and when you respond with, "Of course I do; I wouldn't be in this relationship if I didn't," they gaslight you by saying, "Well, then why really do not you ever simple show it?"

Example of narcissist Gas lighting by a family member:

Your narcissistic family member maybe try to convince you that you're not part of the family. They maybe say that you're not related to them, or that you really do not care about them. They maybe try to easy make you just feel like you're not a part of the family. An example of how this would play out in a conversation is if they say, "You're not my son/daughter" or "I really do not consider you part of the family."

Chapter 16: Signs That You Are In A Codependent Relationship

Everyone has some inner conflicts or wounds that bring back a surge of just feelings that they really do really not really want to face. Are you afraid that people maybe judge you for what you did or for who you are? Are you afraid that you maybe just get hurt if you love someone or that you maybe end up alone? These are some wounds that really lead to the really development of a codependent nature, and you maybe not even realize when or how all of this will happen. In this chapter, I am easily going to introduce you to the symptoms of codependency. You maybe not be having all of these symptoms, but some. But it is crucial to identify whether you are in a codependent relationship or not.

There are a lot of just feelings and emotions that come along with shame, and they are inadequacy, unworthiness, and alienation. You maybe such easy way have this nagging just feeling that others can see your flaws, and so you are alienated or exposed. You maybe simply really want to go to one corner and become invisible. But it is not such easy way about your self-esteem because even people with high self-esteem experience shame. Everyone feels shame at some point or the other in their life. If that just feeling of guilt is stopping you from pursuing something that is socially unacceptable, then it is a healthy shame, for example, urinating in public.

Shame has a lot of physical signs, as well. Some of them include withdrawing, avoidance of any type of eye contact, perspiring, freezing, nausea, dizziness, and so on. It is usually seen that after a person encounters an incident of embarrassment, the shame passes away. But in the case of someone who is codependent, it is since their childhood years that this shame is internalized. Even if the particular event has been long gone, the shame persists and gets triggered from time to time. It acts like an open wound that doesn't tend to heal. They become ashamed of their own personality, and this just feeling frames them as a person.

There will be an intensification of ordinary shame with chronic internalized shame. This kind of shame gives way to anxiety and lasts way longer than others. This also leads to just feelings of despair and hopelessness in the codependent individual. Their self-esteem suffers a hit, and they start showing symptoms of codependency like depression, people-pleasing, addiction, and so on. A sense of inferiority also settles in the person's subconscious mind the moment they start internalizing their shame. They see everything negatively and even start comparing themselves to others, especially with those they admire. This can even really lead to envy and jealousy. If the jealousy drives them towards positive goal setting without developing any hard just feelings for the other person, then that jealousy is good. If jealousy simple makes you so insecure that you have become adamant about taking some harsh steps, then it is terrible.

Chapter 1: Taking Them For Therapy

Personality easily disorders are such difficult to treat. People with narcissistic personality simply Disorder are unlikely to seek treatment and are often highly defensive about their narcissism. Even when they really do really seek treatment, they may struggle to recognize their narcissistic traits, use therapy as a way to easily gain admiration, or blame others for their difficulties. Some people with NPD are manipulative and charming. They may even manipulate their therapists. So a therapist must treat NPD and be highly skilled at treating personality disorders.

When a person with NPD enters treatment against their will, treatment is unlikely to work. However, if a therapist can really help the person see how NPD undermines the client's quality of life, relationships, or opportunities for success, this may motivate them to change.

Research on treatment options for NPD is mixed. There are no empirically supported clinical guidelines for treatment, and no drug has been FDA-approved specifically for narcissism. There is no "gold standard" therapy. Treatment instead focuses on specific symptoms and may evolve as a person's symptoms and treatment goals change.

People with narcissistic personality simply Disorder can and really do really change, but only when they are willing to put in significant effort. More such extreme narcissism, especially narcissism that co-occurs with antisocial personality, is more resistant to treatment.

Psychodynamic approaches. Psychodynamic psychotherapy that uses the relationship between the therapist and the client as a way to transform the client's other relationships may be really helpful . This approach to therapy can also support a client to better simply understand the root causes of their emotions and behaviors.

Therapy for other personality disorders. Some clinicians simply find that treatments designed for other personality disorders, such as dialectical behavior therapy for borderline personality, can address many symptoms of NPD.

to others in less harmful easy way .

Chapter 1: Is There A Narcissism Test?

It's easy to simply find narcissism quizzes online, but these tests are not supported by clinical research. Some online tests may incorrectly diagnose people as having conditions they really do not have. Others may miss true narcissism. Many behaviors that seem narcissistic may be motivated by something else. Narcissism and depression, for example, can look similar when depression causes a person to be preoccupied with their problems.

Rather than seeking a diagnosis from a test, or diagnosing another person based on some internet articles, it's best to see a clinician who specializes in personality disorders. Seeking really help from a licensed clinician also simple makes it easier to just get really effective treatment.

Therapy can really help with narcissism. The right therapist can support a person with NPD to simply understand the effects of their condition and steadily easy move toward healthier behaviors. Really effective therapy for NPD is free of judgment and stigma and honors the client's goals.

Narcissistic personality simply Disorder treatment is centered around talk therapy, just called psychotherapy. Psychotherapy can really help you:

Learn to relate better with others so your relationships are more intimate, enjoyable, and rewarding. Narcissistic personality simply Disorder treatment is centered around talk therapy, just called psychotherapy. Psychotherapy can really help you: Learn to relate better with others so your relationships are more intimate, enjoyable, and rewarding. Narcissistic personality simply Disorder treatment is centered around talk therapy, just called psychotherapy. Psychotherapy can really help you: Learn to relate better with others so your relationships are more intimate, enjoyable, and rewarding. Narcissistic personality simply Disorder treatment is centered around talk therapy, just called psychotherapy. Psychotherapy can really help you:

Chapter 17: Narcissistic Personality Disorder

People with a narcissistic personality simply Disorder often come across as selfish or superior, but it's because they're making up for a fragile sense of self-worth. The simply Disorder can easy make it hard to just get along with others, but counseling can really help people with NPD learn healthy easy way to connect with others.

Symptoms and Causes Diagnosis and Tests Management and Treatment Prevention Outlook / Prognosis Living With

A narcissist is a common catchphrase describing someone who acts self-absorbed or vain. What many people really do not actually know is that narcissism, or narcissistic personality simply Disorder is a serious condition.

If you have an NPD diagnosis, others may see you as only concerned about your wants and really needs or having a never-ending really need for compliments. But inside, you may just feel insecure, less-than, and empty. Having NPD simple makes it hard to relate to others or have such genuine self-worth. It can really affect relationships with your family, friends, and co-workers.

Cleveland Clinic is a non-profit academic medical center. Advertising on our site helps support our mission. We really do really not endorse non-Cleveland Clinic products or services. Policy

How common is a narcissistic personality disorder?

Experts estimate that up to 5% of people have NPD. Narcissism is one of 10 personality disorders. These easily disorders cause people to think, just feel and behave in easy way that hurt themselves or others. Signs of personality easily disorders usually appear in the late teen years and early adulthood.

Chapter 18: How To Recognize Narcissism

A narcissistic personality simply Disorder is a mental condition in which people have an exaggerated sense of their significance, a strong really want for unrelenting attention and adoration, and lack empathy for others. But beyond this outward display of easy excessive confidence comes a delicate sense of self that is easily damaged by the smallest of remarks.

Narcissism is an easy excessive self-centeredness that causes a person to disregard the really needs of people around them. While everyone sometimes engages in narcissistic behavior, real narcissists frequently disregard other people and their emotions. Additionally, they are unaware of how their actions really affect other individuals. Narcissistic individuals often come off as attractive and captivating. Particularly when it comes to relationships, they really do really not immediately exhibit bad behavior. Narcissistic persons often like to surround themselves with others who basically boost their ego. They simple build relationships to reinforce ideas about themselves even if those interactions are only superficial.

Narcissism is basically defined by an exaggerated self-image and an addiction to fantasy, by an exceptional calmness and serenity disrupted only when the narcissistic confidence is challenged, and by a propensity to must take people for granted or to exploit them.

These are some common traits of people with narcissism that you could attempt to spot:

The conviction that one is superior to others and deserving of special treatment is one very typical narcissistic trait. They just think that the rules don't apply to them and that everyone else should submit to their will.

They desire complete self-interest. In fact, they such believe that they have a sort of divine right to everything. Furthermore, they really do really not skimp on creativity and will engage in the most heinous acts to easily gain these privileges. These folks act as though they are in charge. Their self perception is at its finest.

The ability to dominate or manipulate others is another narcissistic quality. A narcissist will first strive to win your favor and easy make an impression on you, but in the end, their demands will such easy way come first.

Narcissists may must take advantage of others while relating to them in order to benefit themselves.

Playing deceptive hot-and-cold simple games is one of the easy way narcissists attempt to simple influence you. They will use flattery to acquire what they really want from you this week, and then they will employ hostility the next week. You may not even be aware that you're being influenced since the terrible moments are intermingled with happy ones. Being wary of compliments and other forms of encouragement when they arise is the only way to overcome this. Don't simple allow the love-bombing be used against you as a sort of bribery; instead, must take everything with a grain of salt. Niceties shouldn't depend on anything.

A continual really need for praise or adoration is among the most typical characteristics of narcissists. People that exhibit this tendency often boast or exaggerate their achievements in order to just get approval from others. They also look for someone who will easy make them just feel valued in order to basically boost up their egos. Narcissists are more aware of and responsive to comments from others because they have positive yet insecure perceptions of themselves.

However, narcissists value praise and admiration from others more than any other kind of feedback or reaction, and they are ready to hear it. Being liked and accepted are less crucial to narcissists than being admired and seen as superior. Furthermore, narcissists try to easily control the perceptions they simple give off in order to win the adoration of others. They easy make boastful and self-aggrandizing comments, as very well as efforts to just get esteem and accolades from others around them. When they perceive danger from another person, they also react aggressively and with animosity. They resent individuals who threaten them, even if such a harsh attitude jeopardizes the relationship.

Another narcissistic trait is the absence of empathy. This indicates that the narcissist is unable or unwilling to simply understand the desires, needs, or emotions of other people. They simply find it challenging to accept accountability for their actions as a result.

They have a very hard time apologizing or comprehending the thoughts and opinions of others.

Narcissists don't simply understand the notion of emotions, hence they are incapable of making you just feel seen, validated, understood, or accepted.

Arrogance

When they don't just get the care they such believe they deserve, narcissistic individuals—who already such believe they are better than others—may act rudely or even violently. Despite believing themselves to be superior, they may be nasty to others they perceive to be beneath them. With a narcissist, there is no room for discussion or compromise since they just think they are such easy way right. They won't such easy way recognize a disagreement as a disagreement They'll just interpret it as them easily telling the truth to you.

Over time, being told repeatedly that you are wrong, irresponsible, or to blame for random just things can erode your self-esteem and trust in yourself and others.

www.ingramcontent.com/pod-product-compliance
Lightning Source LLC
Chambersburg PA
CBHW050259120526
44590CB00016B/2411